One to One Plant Problem Solver

JERRY BAKER
The American Master Gardener

Baronet Publishing Company • *New York*

ONE-TO-ONE PLANT PROBLEM SOLVER

A Baronet Book

First Baronet Printing February 1979

Copyright © 1979 Jerry Baker

ISBN: 0-89437-051-0

TEXT DESIGN BY DENNIS J. GRASTORF

Printed in the USA

BARONET PUBLISHING COMPANY
509 Madison Avenue
New York, N.Y. 10011

TOO OFTEN, most of us select plants for home or office on impulse. In some cases, the selection is based upon the style or color of container the plant is in, or the color of foliage and blooms. In others, the choice is made by the size of plant, shape of foliage, or even just plain price.

When a plant is purchased for a girlfriend, client or boss, for instance, the most expensive is a must. But if it is bought for an office, modest apartment, or home, "big and cheap" is usually the order of the day. Seldom, if ever, do professionals—interior designers, florists and decorators—take into consideration the psychological repercussions of making an improper choice of plant and container for an indoor environment. But our house plants do affect the way we live and the way we feel.

As the popularity of growing plants increases, another serious problem concerning plant and people compatibility arises more and more frequently. We call it "the black thumb syndrome," which can be translated as: "Nothing will grow for me" or "Everything I touch dies." A plant's physical discomfort—unsuitable temperature, humidity, air circulation, light, feeding or watering, which usually results from a gardener's lack of basic information about the plant's growing requirements, combined with a clash of personalities between plant and person—makes the plant's increasing unhealthiness inevitable. A plant needing special and frequent care in the company of a person with little patience is a fatal combination. Likewise, too big a plant for a gardener of slight stature oftentimes ends up in disaster.

This "One-to-One" guide is designed to give you a basic understanding of the proper selection, cause, effect, care and cure of house plants.

These are the same questions that I would ask if you were to call, and likewise with the answers.

INSTRUCTIONS

On a separate piece of paper simply write down the numbers of the questions with the letter(s) that most nearly describe you (in Part I), and your available growing conditions and present plant appearances (in Part II).

EXAMPLE:

Part I	Part II
1-a	1-a
2-b	7-c,d
3-c	21-b
4-c	

Next simply compare your list with the appropriate number in each section and the letter designation. You will find a compatible selection of plants for your "Green Theme," as well as sound guidance on the prevention and cure of plant problems.

NOTE: Please be sure to read any opening paragraph that is not designated a, b, or c in connection to any of your question selections.

PART ONE

Putting Together Your "Green Theme"

LET'S GET PERSONAL

1. Sex
   a. male
   b. female

2. Age
   a. 18-25
   b. 25-35
   c. 35-50
   d. over 50

3. Marital Status
   a. married
   b. single
   c. divorced
   d. widowed

4. Dependents
   a. children

   b. relatives
   c. pets

5. Income
   a. fixed
   b. middle
   c. upper

6. Coloring
   a. light
   b. medium
   c. dark

1

Whether you are male or female makes a great deal of difference in the type of plant selection: foliage, flowering, or special foliage.

a. Men as a rule are partial to flowering and colorful foliage plants because of the challenge in growing and maintaining them. Such flowering plants as orchids, violets, miniature roses, gloxenias, bromeliads, mums and geraniums are the favorites, while croton, rex begonias and coleus with their beautiful foliage are not far behind.

b. Women, on the other hand, fall in love with darn near any plant that bears a flower, or berry, but they do not always end up buying such varieties. When it comes right down to making a purchase, women tend to go for such foliage plants as ferns, vines, ivys and corn plants. Esthetics holds second place to simple care and longevity.

2

Your age has a great deal to do with what plant varieties are right for you.

a. 18-25-year-old females can add to their apartment any plant they can afford if the indoor environment will be compatible with the plant's needs. Males in this age bracket are best advised to admire the females' plant collections and green thumbing.

b. 25-35 is an age range when both sexes have less time for plants as a result of increasing responsibilities. Fortunately, our previously disinterested male finds plant care a new and rewarding hobby that he can afford and enjoy. Most small greenhouses and homemade kits are purchased by men in this age bracket.

c. 35-50 finds an environmental harmony

developing between the male and female, as they have created a successful life together. Both sexes begin to expand their plant tending capabilities. Men lean towards learning special techniques of cross-pollinating and specially breeding rarer varieties, while women broaden plant purchases to include plants that require more time and attention. The flowering house plants and the attractive multifoliage groups merit their keen concern.

d. Over 50 are the top notchers, both male and female, who by this time have learned the secret of green thumb success: Pride, Patience, and Persistence. They can tackle any plant variety they so chose, since they have learned not to take foolish chances with plants for which they do not have the right growing conditions.

3

a. Married males who display an interest in plants generally like to grow bigger and more beautiful flowers than their neighbor, or to produce vegetables from seed to save money. Bromeliads and orchids fill the bill nicely.

Married females as a rule are conservative in their plant selection. They like plants that almost look out for themselves, requiring little extra care or expenditure. Sometimes, they do not attempt more than sticking a broken stem or leaf in a glass of water to root, or dropping orange, grapefruit or lemon seeds in a pot of soil. Very few married women take a serious interest in plant propagation or seedling production because of precious little free time. Best bets, therefore, for this group include such carefree plants as hoya, artillery plant, asparagus fern, inch plants, wandering jews, wax begonias, pothos, spider plant, prayer plant, and sansevieria.

b. Single males do not for the most part take a serious interest in plants for their apartments. Those who do fancy plants prefer large, hardy foliage plants such as dracena, plandanus, veitchir and schefflera, philodendron selloum, and the old standby, sansevieria. Even plastic plants are not out of the question for this group.

Single females are, on the whole, garden plant enthusiasts. They experiment with all kinds of plant material. They are not afraid to fail, and over time, they learn from their mistakes to create a dazzling array of windowsill greenery.

c. Divorced males in their first eighteen months to two years are generally hopeless cases when it comes to plant caretaking. I highly recommend floral paintings and artificial plants rather than torturing the poor live ones. The exception seems to be that many newly single males show an interest in the cactus family, but they are careful not to get another "thorn in the side."

Divorced females, on the other hand, may seize upon plant growing as therapeutic relief, and they may exhibit the same interest in plants as do younger single females. Particularly pleasing plants to soothe feelings include strawberry begonias, wax begonias, prayer plants, and violets.

d. The widower generally becomes responsible for tending his deceased wife's prized and loved plant collection. More often than not, he is at a loss as to where to begin. To give the plants away would bring a rush of guilt.

In most situations, fortunately, the widower comes to view taking care of the plants as a continuation of his nurturant feelings for his wife. Those plants which do not do well, however, become candidates for gifts to friends or relatives with a greater degree of green thumb ability. But those that succeed give him a feeling of great pride. He recognizes the smiling face of his wife and the fond memories of their life together as her plants live on.

Widowed females tend to give more attention to their plants and to show new interest in propagation of their plants and in cuttings. If their husbands had a plant hobby, they will generally dive headlong into where he left off.

4

a. Families with children restrict their selection, as a rule, to plants that are safe, hardy and mostly self-sufficient: pothos, philodendron, piggyback, peperomia, dracena, schefflera, sansevieria and hoya, wandering jew and asparagus fern. Once the children remain in school most of the day, you will find that your interest and time will enable you to expand your plant collection.

b. Parents can be both a help and a hindrance. On many occasions, they will offer the same degree of green thumb advice as they do with child rearing. It won't hurt to listen from time to time. You will actually be delighted to see how both the quality and quantity of your plant family improves when a senior citizen is permitted to share in your green thumb experience.

c. Pets are dependents and must be considered when selecting plants. Cats are attracted to hanging vines and soft moving foliage like aralia, Norfolk pines, and palms. It is more important that you do not place a plant in a pet's favorite lounging spot whatever the plant may be.

5

As you no doubt have already discovered, house plants are no longer cheap. With the increased interest in plants, their prices have risen. This is basic supply and demand. Your income will have a great deal to do, therefore, with the sizes and varieties you are able to afford. My first and most sincere suggestion to all of you is to join a local garden club or start one of your own. This will give you an opportunity to learn and trade with other members, which will keep your cost down and your plant possibilities up.

a. If you are on a low or fixed income, my suggestion is that you mix economy, practicality, and imagination by considering growing vegetables as house plants. Peppers, tomatoes, and cucumbers will do for a start. So save those avacado pits, orange, lemon and lime seeds. If you live near a forest area, another money saving plant idea would be to plant evergreen cuttings from any of the Junipers. These make super plants and you look like a super green thumb.

In buying plants, you should stick to the big ten in house plants: grape ivy, sansevieria, philodendron ivy, marantha, fern, wandering jew, piggyback, pothos, wax begonias, and African violets.

b. Don't let your income fool you into thinking you can easily become a green thumber. In nine out of ten cases, what counts is appreciating the plant and the investment in it whatever your income level. Any and all of the above plants can become part of your plant family. Even though they have been suggested for those with limited means, they are not to be stigmatized as plants for paupers. But with more spare cash to invest, the medium income person can more easily afford almost any of the nearly 5,000 varieties of plants on the market. Take a careful look at:

1. CACTUS—Golden lace, spider aloe, jade plant, Mexican giant, bunny ears, duck wings and panda plant.

2. SUCCULENTS—Aloe vera, donkey tail, necklace vine, wax flower and rosary vine.

3. COLOR FOLIAGE—Copper leaf, Merry

Christmas begonia, rex begonia, caladrum, peacock plant, croton, coleus, trielime begonia, Hawaiian ti, seersucker plant, velvet plant and arrowroot, peperomia, burgundy philodendron, soffrom pepper, panemiga, purple heart.

C. Where money is no object, the selection is unlimited. Odds are you have more space, and you will be able to purchase larger, more mature plants. Make sure that the plant foliage, color and size complement your decor. Here are a few plants that will be conversation pieces: Calico hearts, pretty pebbles, sea shells, colored eggs, cattail cactus, foxtail fern, elephant food, old man cactus, stag horn fern, olive, indoor oak, moonstones, pan amiga, orchids, Chinese podcarpus, spider brake fern, rice paper plant, Ming arolia, dragon plant.

6

a. Your personal environment includes the spaces where you work, live, and play. They should, where possible, be decorated to make you feel comfortable and relaxed as well as secure. When you are selecting plants for your Green theme, make sure that you stand near a mirror. See how the depth of color of the foliage contrasts with your hair and skin coloring. If you are light or pale complected, do not select foliage or flowering plants that are lighter than your complexion. If you do, you will look washed out next to your plants. Also, you should pay attention to your undertones—pink, yellow, olive or tan. Choosing plants that are compatible with skin coloration will make you feel the happiest as they will enhance your appearance.

b. If you are of medium complexion, you need not pay special attention to your coloring in selecting your plant friends.

25

C. If your complexion is dark, you should avoid plants the hue of which is darker than your skin. Stay with plants that have leaves in lighter shades of green.

PART TWO

Keeping Your "Green Scene" Green

WHERE DO YOU LIVE

1. Is your home
    a. urban
    b. rural
    c. suburban

2. In what section of the country do you live?
    a. northern
    b. southern

3. Do you live near a large body of water?
    a. no
    b. yes
    c. do not know

4. What kind of water do you have?
    a. hard
    b. soft
    c. do not know

YOUR HOME OR APARTMENT

5. Are the exterior walls of your home or apartment house
   a. brick or concrete
   b. wood
   c. metal-sided

6. Are the interior walls of your home
   a. paneled
   b. plaster or plaster board
   c. natural, untreated

7. Are the walls and ceilings of your home insulated?
   a. yes
   b. no

8. What kind of heating system do you have?
   a. gas
   b. oil
   c. coal or wood
   d. electric

9. The windows of your house or apartment face which direction? (check several if necessary)

   a. north
   b. south
   c. east
   d. west

10. Would you describe the rooms as (check several if necessary)
   a. bright and sunny
   b. moderately lighted by daylight
   c. dark

11. What is the average year-round temperature of your home?
   a. 74°-up
   b. 68°-73°
   c. below 68°

12. Do you run (check several if necessary)
   a. a humidifier
   b. a dehumidifier
   c. air conditioning
   d. none of the above

13. Do you supplement your plants' lighting with artificial light?
   a. yes
   b. no

14. Do you usually keep some windows open?
    a. yes
    b. no

15. In what areas of your home would you like to add plants or improve on the ones you have now?
    a. living room
    b. dining room
    c. kitchen
    d. bathroom
    e. bedroom
    f. hallway

16. In what kind(s) of house plants are you interested? (check several if necessary)
    a. foliage
    b. cacti
    c. flowering
    d. varied

YOUR PLANT AND YOU

17. How much time per day do you have available for your plants?
    a. a few minutes
    b. as much time as necessary
    c. more time than I need

18. How many people are there in your home?
    a. one
    b. 2-5
    c. 6 or more

19. Do you have young children in the family?
    a. yes
    b. no

20. Is your house or apartment usually
    a. quiet
    b. noisy

CARING FOR YOUR PLANT

21. Do you have smokers in the family?
    a. yes
    b. no

22. Did you acquire your plants as
    a. gifts
    b. purchases
    c. both of the above

23. Why do you have plants?
    a. I enjoy them
    b. they are fashionable
    c. they were gifts

24. Do you (check several if necessary)
    a. talk to your plants
    b. name your plants
    c. play music for your plants
    d. none of the above

25. Do you (check several if necessary)
    a. touch or turn your plants
    b. vibrate your plants
    c. move your plants
    d. none of the above

26. When one of your plants seems unhealthy,
    do you
    a. do nothing
    b. throw it away
    c. look for the problem
    d. consult a spouse, friend, or book

27. How often do you feed your house plants?
    a. once a day
    b. once a week
    c. once a month
    d. four times a year
    e. never

28. How often do you water your house plants?

a. once a day
b. once a week
c. when the soil feels dry

29. Do you (check several if necessary)
    a. mist your foliage
    b. wash the leaves of your foliage plants
    c. insect spray or dust your plants

30. Do you
    a. buy potting soil
    b. prepare your own potting soil

31. In what kinds of pots are your house plants
    (check several if necessary)
    a. clay
    b. ceramic or china
    c. plastic
    d. wood
    e. metal

32. Do your house plant pots have holes in the
    bottom?
    a. yes
    b. no
    c. some do and some don't

33. Are pots resting on an underliner (a separate saucer, tray, etc.)?
    a. yes
    b. no

SYMPTOMS & CONDITIONS

34. Does the crust of the soil or do your pots show signs of (check several if necessary)
    a. green moss
    b. white crystals or grayish power
    c. none of the above

35. Do you notice (check several if necessary)
    a. insects on the foliage
    b. insects on the stems and/or the surface of the soil
    c. curled-up leaves
    d. mold
    e. holes
    f. none of the above

36. How would you describe the shape of your house plants?
    a. tall with sparse foliage
    b. dwarfed with thick foliage
    c. full and well-shaped

37. Have you noticed that your plants have

(check several if necessary)
a. scaly or cracking foliage
b. light green leaves with dark green veins
c. beads of moisture on the surface of the leaves

38. Do your house plants lose leaves from
    a. new growth at the top
    b. the middle to lower foliage
    c. neither of the above

39. How would you describe the coloring of your house plants' foliage?
    a. rich and bright
    b. off-color, faded or yellow

40. Are the tips of the leaves
    a. brown
    b. black
    c. consistent with the color (s) of the leaves

41. Do the leaves of your house plants tend to (check several if necessary)
    a. stand out firmly
    b. wilt or droop
    c. have brown or black spots
    d. be dull

1

Like most humans, plants enjoy life in the country best, the suburbs next. They only live in cities to please and accompany you. Since you live where you do, let's review together the peculiarities of your environment that affect the health and happpiness of your house plants and you, too.

a. Living in the city, your plants will require closer supervision than their suburban or country cousins, particularly because of air pollution. Cigarette, cigar, and pipe smoke kill plants, and with city traffic and industrial exhaust, your plants are especially in need of some TLC (tender loving care). Wash the foliage and mist frequently. You should also know that constant street noises make it just as difficult for your plants to rest as it is for you to get a good night's sleep—and your plants need their rest. Do both of you a favor and block off the outside noise pollution for part of the time. Another consideration of city living is that of building reflection. When figuring out lighting needs for your plants, don't forget the effects of light reflection. Light reflecting off a nearby building is often as good as direct light. But the reverse is also true; a nearby dark building can block off the natural light. You can't judge lighting by a clock alone. Street lights, and bright signs will also affect your plants' health.

b. Living in the country, your house plants won't require as close supervision as their city cousins, particularly because you live in a clean air environment—at least for now, but beware of heavy tobacco smoke. Since there are many more insects in your environs than in a city, there's a good chance a few will try to make a home in the soil from your backyard for potting house plants, unless you sterilize it first. If you buy sterilized, packaged soil for potting, you won't have to worry about possible contamination.

c. Living in the suburbs, your plants won't require as close supervision as their city cousins, particularly because the air pollution in your environment is still slightly less than in the cities. However, even suburbs have traffic problems, and the exhaust from city industries drifts pretty far. Since smoke exhaust kills plants, be safe rather than sorry. Wash the foliage and mist regularly to ensure clean and pollution-free plants. Also keep an eye out for insects who decide to make your plants their home. When repotting your house plants, avoid using the soil from your backyard. Your plants won't have to worry about possible contamination if potted in sterilized, packaged soil.

2

I guess it's no surprise when I say that your geographical location does make some difference in the care and available selection of your house plants, though, admittedly, today anything is possible.

a. Living in the north, my biggest concern is winter purchases of plants. Try not to buy a new plant when the temperature is freezing or below and you're alone with no one to keep the car warm and hold the plant on the way home. Be sure to have the clerk carefully bag the plant and seal it, if possible. Most local nurseries and garden centers will only carry area-tolerant plants. Therefore, if you purchase a house plant locally, you can be sure the plant can at least potentially adjust to your living conditions.

b. Living in the south, I'd advise you to keep

a close eye on the air conditioner to maintain the recommended comfort zone: 70°-74° F. Be sure to keep plants out of direct cool drafts. Since the sun in the south rises higher in the sky and is hotter than it is in the north, a plant growing in a window with southern exposure can easily get more sun than it likes and be burned. You might want to shade such a window with sheer curtains.

3

Moisture in the atmosphere, or humidity, is just as good for your plants as it is for you. For me, you ask? If you don't believe me, just check the counters where beauty preparations are sold and count the number of "moistures!" Phyllis Philodendron doesn't want wrinkled, dry skin on her leaves any more than you do. My advice is to take away the guesswork and know the amount of moisture in your home by purchasing a hydrometer or an inexpensive humidity gauge at your hardware store. More on humidity later.

a. Since you do not live near a large body of water, which would aid in maintaining a high humidity level, take extra care to have enough moisture in your home so your plants and you will stay comfortable and at your beautiful best. You might want to purchase a mechanical humidifier, or even a baby's vaporizer which will humidify a single room.

b. Since you live near a large body of water, you'll probably have less trouble maintaining proper humidity than if you lived on the desert, at least on days when the wind blows in your direction. But if you live near salt water, be sure to wash the leaves of your plants regularly. The airborne mists carry enough salt to harm plants.

c. Since you aren't sure whether or not you live near a large body of water, you can't use that knowledge to help determine the humidity level in your home. In that case, I'd urge you to invest in a hydrometer, as I mentioned above, or at least listen to your local weather reports over a month's time so you get an idea of what the humidity in your area is like.

4

The type of water you use does make a difference. Plants prefer hard water, rain water, or water from an air conditioner or refrigerator. Although most plants aren't too particular, room temperature water is ideal for all, and African violets and poinsettias, especially, will cringe if given an icy bath or drink. If you like to set your house plants outside when it rains, remember that a driving rain or cooler outdoor temperatures than indoors can destroy your plants. Why not catch the rain water in containers and store it for later use on your plants? Tap water or water containing a water softener should be filtered through agricultural charcoal before being given to your plants, in order to remove harmful salts and chemicals. Since plants don't have teeth, they don't need flouride. You can filter the water separately, or you can filter and water at the same time by placing a thin layer of agricultural charcoal over the surface of the soil.

47

a. The main problem with hard water, which you have, is that it has a heavy salt content, harmful to your plants, especially African violets, and destructive to clay pots! Azaleas, gardenias and camillias, too, hate salt, so take time to filter your water, and then you won't have to worry who likes what.

b. Since your water is soft, which means chemicals have been added to it, you have no choice but to filter it through agricultural charcoal. Otherwise, you're causing almost as much trouble as you're eliminating each time you water!

c. Since you aren't sure whether your water is hard or soft, take time to filter it through agricultural charcoal. Then you can't go wrong.

5

From your house plants' point of view, a greenhouse is the ideal living environment. But then, most realize this is impossible and are willing to compromise if you'll take proper steps to ensure an even temperature the year round.

a. Brick or concrete homes or apartment buildings are the easiest for plants. They retain the heat in winter and coolness in summer. Keep your eye on the thermostats of your air conditioner and furnace to maintain temperatures approximating 72° during the day and 68° at night.

b. Wood frame homes and apartment buildings have a tendency to cool off quickly and heat up in hot weather. Because of this fluctuation, you'll have to keep close watch on the thermostats of both your air conditioner and furnace to maintain an even temperature approximating 72° during the day and 68° at night.

C. Metal-sided homes or apartment buildings are easy on plants. They retain the heat in winter and coolness during summer. Keep your eye on the thermostats of your air conditioner and furnace to maintain temperatures approximating 72° during the day and 68° at night.

6

You're wondering why I'd ask a foolish question like "What kind of walls do you have?" The type of walls, I'd answer, as well as carpeting, window covers, upholstery and draperies in your home all have a bearing on your plants' health and happiness.

a. Paneled walls of any kind are hard-surfaced and do not hold much moisture. Likewise, wood, chrome and glass, plastic or nylon furnishings don't hold moisture either. To compensate, you'll need to add humidity to your home earlier in the fall than a neighbor with plaster walls and cotton or wool upholstery and drapes. Surprised?

b. Plaster or plaster board walls retain moisture for a longer period of time than wood. Nonporous paneling holds no moisture. Wool and cotton fabrics hold more moisture than non-porous sythetics; likewise, upholstered furniture holds more moisture than wood or chrome and glass furnishings. If you've mixed plaster walls with a fair amount of "breathing" furnishings, humidity control in your home will be minimal. Your home will be humid until it begins to get really cold, when you'll begin adding humidity to the environment. Surprised?

C. Natural, untreated wood and brick walls retain moisture for a longer period of time than does non-porous wooden or plastic paneling. Wool and cotton fabrics hold more moisture than non-porous synthetics; likewise, upholstered furnishings hold more moisture than wood or chrome and glass furnishings. If you've complemented your walls with a fair amount of "breathing" furnishings, humidity control in your home will be minimal. Your home will be humid until it begins to get really cold, when you'll have to begin adding humidity to the environment. Surprised?

7

Earlier on, I referred to the fact that plants don't like sudden changes in temperature any more than you do. An even temperature or comfort zone is ideal for you both.

a. Your insulation will help you maintain the even temperature that you and your plants should have with minimum adjusting of your thermostat, or of other temperature controls in your home.

b. Your lack of insulation leaves your home vulnerable to sudden changes in temperature. If you find these sharp changes uncomfortable, so do your plants. This means more work for you in watching the thermometer and adjusting your thermostat or other temperature control units more frequently in order to keep a relatively even temperature range in the house. Be particu-

larly careful to keep your plants out of drafts.
You wouldn't want to spend 24 hours a day
sitting in a draft, and plants are as sensitive
as you are.

8

Though manufacturers of heating equipment and we homeowners do our best, we frequently fall short of turning our homes into a plant Shangri-La. Perhaps the task is too tough. There are, however, a number of considerations we should bear in mind to give our indoor plants a helping hand. The type of transmission you have—steam, forced air or radiant—doesn't make much difference. What does make a difference is the location of the heat vents. Since heat rises, make sure that your plants are not put directly under, in front of, or on top of heat ducts, as this will cause the foliage and stems to turn brown and dry out. The same consideration applies to air conditioning in reverse. House plants find rising, warm drafts or sinking cold ones equally distasteful. If you supplement your heat or please your aesthetic taste with an old fashioned wood-burning fireplace, remember that an open fire will quickly dry out your indoor air, and it may spread soot. Try to humidify your plants' immediate environment, and wash their leaves frequently. Some of the sturdiest, easy-to-care for plants are the fiddle leaf fig, rubber plant, iron cross and rex begonia, cast-iron plant, parlour plant and umbrella plant. These are excellent choices for offices as well as homes in which growing conditions are usually ideal and weekend temperature drops are not uncommon.

a. The combustion of natural gas is purer than the combustion of any other fuel available to homeowners today, but it's imperative you be constantly on the alert for leakage. A gas leak will kill you—to say nothing of your house plants! Thick-leaved foliage house plants are best adapted to occasional gas fumes. Avoid all flowering plants except impatiens and billbergia.

b. Oil heat can and does, from time to time, put a film—something like cigarette smoke—on the foliage. Therefore, I'd recommend frequent washings of your house plant foliage.

c. Coal or wood heating has its advantages.

Resulting soot or ash can be used as soil conditioners for potting soil or gardens. However, this type of heating fluctuates more than others, and frequently areas close to the furnace are warmer than areas further away. Make sure the placement of your plants is in keeping with their temperature needs.

d. Though pure, electric heat is bone dry. Keep plants away from the unit or air vents so their foliage will not scorch or wither. Try adding some humidity to your home to compenste for the dryness. Some plants that do well under dry conditions are: aechmea, billbergia, chlorophytium, clivia grevillea, pilea, sansevieria, zebrina, cacti and succulents.

9

No matter what exposure to natural light you have to offer your house plants, there's a variety for you!

a. Your northern exposure is great for begonias, ferns and arabas, as well as for any other shade-loving plant. Foliage plants such as English ivy, philodendron, wandering Jew, and snake or spider plants do well if there is full light during the sun-shining hours.

b. Southern exposure is comfortable for most plants and flowering house plants will bloom in a south window. Remember not to place your plants too close to azaleas, crocus, lilies, daffodils, geraniums, gardinias, hydrangia, pepper plants or morning glories.

c. Muhammadans and house plants share an

affinity for the East. An eastern exposure is the place to be if you're a plant—any plant! Those plants needing no more than four hours of sun a day do best. Try African violets, cyclamens, primroses or ivy.

d. Western exposure is best only for cacti and succulent plants. Remember, here, too, you can't put the plants too close to a curtainless window or they'll surely cook!

10

Plants have 20/20 vision and can see where they're going if there is ample light. Like people though, if you dim the light or leave them in darkness they're liable to stumble or fall and get hurt as they extend their limbs. I recommend supplementing the short daylight hours by running a 60-75 watt soft white light.

a. A bright and sunny room is appropriate for cacti and blooming plants of all kinds. But don't invite tropical foliage plants or most of the ferns to stay! Most begonias, gloxinia, orchids and geraniums will appreciate their surroundings and show it in their growth.

b. The medium natural light you have is perfect for almost all my plant friends. May you and they grow well! African violets, rex begonia, cissus, episcia and syngonium will feel as comfortable in your home as you do.

C. A dark (but not in darkness) room will suit Freda Fern and the Scindapsus family, which includes devil's ivy, ivy arum, and pothos. Aspidistra, dracaena, philodendron and peperomia will also live their happy life.

11

You must think I've talked "comfort zone" 'til I'm (you're) blue in the face, but it really is the most important consideration of your house plants' health and happiness.

a. Since the average year-round temperature of your home is 74° or above, both you and your house plants will perspire and dry out, and long for more than one shower per day. With a high daytime temperature, your house plants will be grateful if you can lower the temperature to 68° during the night. You may find you wake up refreshed and invigorated, too. Especially after you see the lowered cost of your next fuel bill. If you still prefer high room temperatures, then purchase plants which have the same level of heat appreciation that you do. There are many attractive plants in the Bromeliad family. These plants thrive on warmth, and for them room temperatures can never get too hot. They retain water well, and are not bothered by the low humidity in most homes. They are accustomed to very little light and are ideal for darker rooms. For sunny, hot, dry rooms, try cacti or succulents. You might want to purchase a hostess cart and wheel your plants into a cool room for their nightly beauty rest.

b. With the average year-round temperature of your home between 68° and 74°, you and your plants are, as the younger generation would say, "right on." Most house plants will be happy to share your home.

c. Though an average temperature of 68° or below may be okay for you if you have a sweater on, I haven't seen any knitting patterns on the market for plant sweaters! Have a heart and vary 68° at night with something a bit higher during the day. If you really enjoy the coolness (and with the high cost of fuel more and more of us are beginning to), then I'd advise you to purchase some of the many plants that prefer temperatures below 60° F. Some of these "polar plants" are: acacia, anemone coronaria (poppy anemone), azaleas, cyclamens, camellias, English ivy, lilies, pepper plants, primroses and strawberry geraniums.

12

Humidity is necessary for deterring dehydration of the flesh and respiratory system of both you and your plants. During winter, if you find your nose dry, your mouth feeling like cotton, and your skin taut, there is not enough humidity in the air. If you've been spending your winters suffering from dry skin or bronchial trouble, you can help yourself as well as your plants by increasing humidity. Plants give off water through their leaves, and thus cool the air in the immediate vicinity of the leaf as the water evaporates. If the air around the plant is too dry, the plant may give off more water than it can absorb through its roots, causing wilting. That's the reason why, in most cases, the higher the humidity, the better the plants will grow. The ideal percentage range for you and your plants is 50-85 or 90%. Since this is impractical, a percentage range of 35-45% would be perfect. You can keep track with that inexpensive humidity gauge. If your house is too dry, keep your plants in pots on a metal or plastic tray filled with about an inch of gravel or other stones. Whenever you water your plants, sprinkle a little on the gravel. As this evaporates, it will increase the humidity right around the plant. Make sure that the pots are not actually sitting in the water. You can also spray the plants lightly with water once or twice a day, or keep pans filled with water on nearby radiators.

a. Your plants salute you for your consideration in running a humidifier.

b. If your humidifier keeps your house in the proper humidity range, you and your house plants, as well as your other possessions, will be well served!

c. Air conditioning is a terrific comfort, and central air conditioning, particularly, doesn't cause humidity problems. Remember though, not to put plants directly in front of a blasting air conditioner or the foliage will turn black from freezing. You may find it necessary to add to the humidity of your home. If so, do so.

d. Without a humidifier or air conditioning, you would do well by your plants to take advantage of some of these "humidifying" methods. You can also purchase plants which prefer very dry conditions, such as cacti and bromeliads.

13

Using electric light to supplement the lighting of your house plants will make up for any deficiencies in natural lighting caused by dim windows, dull weather, poor exposure, or the fact that indoor lighting does not equal outdoor light. The amount of artificial lighting required by your plants varies with the type of plant and the season. For the most part, plants require a total of twelve to sixteen hours of light a day to bloom. You only need enough electric light to make up the difference between the total light required by a plant and the length of the day. Some plants require as little as four hours a day of direct sunlight to do well, but appreciate a few additional hours of properly regulated electric lighting. Remember that plants growing in strong light need a higher temperature and more water than those growing in lesser light.

a. Since you do use electric lighting to supplement the natural light, you've probably been enjoying the benefits—more luxurious growth, more blossoms, and, since you are no longer dependent on window-lighting, more plants! But don't get carried away. Plant growth is as dependent on darkness as it is on light. If you give your plants more light than they require, it will actually slow up their growth!

b. This is as good a time as ever to begin increasing your indoor garden by using electric lights to supplement natural lighting. Liven up areas of your home you've previously had to overlook—that unused book shelf, a room divider planter, a space over the kitchen counter, a basement playroom. Consult your local garden supplier for the best plant lighting arrangement to suit your purposes. If you decide to try supplemental lighting, make the change gradually. Plants, like people, are often shocked by sudden changes. And, for a plant, changes in light or temperature are of major concern.

14

Just as we prefer fresh air to stale room air, so do our plant friends. After all, where did the first indoor plants come from but the outdoors! Mild, fresh air is the best thing you can give your plants. Good air circulation can prevent many plant problems, such as certain forms of mildew. Just make sure to keep your "green pets" out of drafts.

a. I'm glad to see you're keeping your plants and yourself clear-headed with fresh air. Be sure to wash the foliage regularly to prevent dust buildup, which clogs up plant pores and can result in serious problems. It is also recommended that a small oscillating fan be used to circulate the air when it is not possible to open the windows.

b. A little fresh air will clear up your head as well as your plants'. You can go outside whenever you want, but since your house plants can't, open up a few windows that don't blow in directly on your green and flowered friends and let your plants enjoy some circulating air, too. If it is not possible to open the windows, use a small oscillating fan to move the air for both yours and your plants' health.

15

To rewrite an old phrase, there's a plant for every room and a room for every plant. Wherever you choose to have your plants, I suggest you have as many as possible. I guess I'm not going to be a big hit with the zero population folks because, like my family of five children, I believe you should have as many house plants as you have the time, patience, income and space for. With proper selection, there is no area of your home which should be without plants, if you want them. Besides their personal, decorative and hobby appeal, plants give off oxygen and keep the air in your home fresh. If you add a half-inch layer of charcoal to the top of the soil in the pots, it will help to remove any unpleasant or lingering odors from cooking or smoking. Most important, they brighten your spirits. Before you set up any plant in residence, check for drafts by placing a candle on a saucer and lighting it. If the flame is blown out or blows in one direction for a long period of time, avoid that spot for your foliage friends, or they'll perish.

a. House plants should enhance the decor of your living room from the standpoint of color, texture and shape. You might want to try a plant window, which is a plant trough running along the full length of a picture window instead of a window sill. A miniature fruit tree can also be a great conversation piece, as can an unused fish tank garden.

b. In your dining room, house plants can be a thing of beauty or a centerpiece on your table (a low, green and white creeper, fittonia, is appropriate, or try a planter of philodendron, dracaena and codiaeum). As in the living room, you'll want plants to enhance your decor. Use them as a divider between living and dining areas. Tetrastigma or cissus antarctia (chestnut or kangaroo vines) provide a dense screen. A small-leafed climber such as Ficus pumila or Hedera helix (climbing fig or ivy) will decorate the supports without cutting the light or hiding the view.

c. House plants in the kitchen can be a special

boon to anyone who spends many hours a day there. Besides brightening your spirits and the room's decor, house plants perspire and share their moisture. Many double as foods, so why not try an indoor vegetable, fruit or window herb garden? Such common vegetables as sweet potatoes, carrots, beets and rutabagas have unusual, interesting foliage, and are simple to grow. Just place a starter vegetable in water and watch it take root. For carrots and rutabagas, take a 3″ cutting from the top, cover all but ¼″-½″ with pebbles, and then cover the pebbles with water. Kitchens are more susceptible to grease and grime than other rooms of the house, so mist and wash your foliage frequently. Be sure to keep them well-watered, and make sure there is enough humidity for their growth. If you use a gas stove, thick-leaved foliage house plants will survive any occasional fumes the best.

d. House plants will love the moist, humid environment of a bathroom, as long as they're varieties requiring little light. Try Freda Fern and the rest of her water-loving family. And remember, with a layer of charcoal in their pots, your ferns will be natural air fresheners!

e. Let me dispel the old wives' tale that says it's dangerous to have house plants in a bedroom, sick room or nursery. Plants exhale oxygen and share their moisture, both of which are beneficial to you. Why not brighten up the room by using plants with colorful foliage? Many plants have multicolored edges or spots. Try sansevieria, peperomia, dracaena, ivy, zebrina, maranta, coleus, rex begonia, conideum or cordyline.

f. House plants can be a solution to hallways you "don't know what to do with." Though most hallways are dark, there are many types of house plants that will do well. Ask your florists or nurseryman about aspidistra, fatsia, ferns, philodendron, hedera, ficus pumila, or maranta. All of these prefer a dim and cool environment.

16

a. Foliage house plants usually grow slowly and change little. By the same token, they are truly permanent residents. Many beginning home gardeners think of foliage plants as "just plain green." Not true! These plants come in all sizes, leaf patterns, and color shadings. Stop by your florist and check out the pileas, coleus and crotons.

b. I think of cacti as the fun members of your indoor garden. Because of their strange and unique shapes and textures, they remind me of prehistoric beasts and reptiles! They're favorites, usually, of children. The varieties and colors are infinite, and the flowers of some cacti are unsurpassed in beauty by orchids. As a cacti grower, you may not need words of warning. But I've found two common misconceptions about growing cacti. First, cacti do not survive in sand alone. While good drainage, which sand and gravel supply, is essential, cacti need a nutritional soil—a mixture of garden loam, leaf mold, and sand or gravel—the way other types of house plants do. Also, cacti grow few roots and should be housed in containers that you may think are too small for the plant—usually about one inch wider than the width of the plant. If you let the roots roam, they'll forget to let the flowers bloom. Repot your cacti in the spring. Newly potted cacti should be kept in a warm, lightly shaded place and watered just enough to dampen the soil, which should be kept damp until growth begins. Cacti rest during the winter, and prefer a cool room. During that time of year water just enough so they don't dry out completely, and only on bright days. During spring and summer you can feed monthly with diluted liquid food and water thoroughly when the surface feels dry. Let the surface dry out completely every now and then to avoid souring the soil.

C. There are flowering house plants and flowering pot plants and bulbs. The former are permanent residents, while varieties of the latter are often moved outside for the summer or fall, and cannot be saved from year to year. In either case, however, the size and color of the blossoms tells you a great deal about what the plant thinks of its location and diet. If the blossoms are pale, your plant is not getting enough light; if they are undersized there is too much nitrogen in their food. Be extra careful to make sure there is sufficient humidity during the time your plant is blooming, and that the plants are well-watered and in containers of the proper size. Plants will not bloom in pots that are too big—they are easily intimidated when they feel lost. You might also add ¼ teaspoon of epsom salts to the surface of the soil of each flowering plant in the fall.

d. You and I agree on having a variety of types of house plants. I could no more be happy having only one category of house plant as I could listening to one type of music! Perhaps for you, now's as good a time as any to make some suggestions for further activities. Have you tried building a terrarium, mini-gardening with vegetables, fruits and herbs, or water gardening in an unused aquarium with aquatic plants? The possibilities are endless and the hobby can be as rich and varied as you make it!

17

I've asked about how much time per day you spend caring for your house plants to get an idea of your interest and involvement, more than anything. Obviously, the number of plants you have and the pressures of other responsibilities will factor in the time spent on plants.

a. Plants are precious and should be treated royally. If you haven't much time for plant care, stay with varieties that will thrive even with little attention. You can even vacation for a few days and come back to find your plants doing fine— only don't stretch their possibilities too far. Try the bromeliads, most of the ivy family, philodendrons, rubber, snake, or spider plants, or some of the succulents. Easy flowering plants are billbergia, clivia, geraniums, impatiens, fuchsia and all of the cactus plants. You might want to save time by using pots with an automatic watering wick in the bottom. Just check occassionally and add water to the surface of the soil at least once or twice a month.

b. Since you have as much time as necessary to care for your plants in the manner they deserve, they should be rewarding your attention with plentiful new growth. If they aren't, take some time to examine the possible reasons for their "non-growth." Part of being a good gardener is recognizing when your plants aren't growing as well as they should. That's a lot more difficult than recognizing an obvious problem. If your plants are doing well, add to your gardening enjoyment and pride by experimenting with "Plant Parenthood," or plant propagation. Try taking cuttings, air layering or dividing plants. Of course, you'll then need more time to take care of all your new plants!

c. Since you have extra time on your hands, why not add to your gardening pride and enjoyment? There are countless gardening projects you can learn to do, ranging from plant propagation—taking cuttings, air layering, grafting and root dividing—to building specialty gardens and growing exotic or delicate varieties of plants.

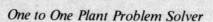

One to One Plant Problem Solver

Home gardening indoors can be a full-time hobby, and besides being challenging and entertaining, it can result in food for your table or gifts for your friends.

18

a. I've found that indoor gardening is one of the most pleasurable and rewarding hobbies for anyone who lives alone. It can take as much time, concentration and concern as you care to give your plants. For example, you can enjoy caring for your plants as you listen to music or watch television. Your plants may prefer it if you do, since they like the media too! On the other hand, you'll find it just as easy to become totally absorbed in tending your plants without the distraction of other things going on in your home. If you treat your plants like the friends they are, just think how pleasant it becomes to come home to a houseful of good friends—friends who won't spend the evening complaining of problems!

b. The more people at home, the more plants you can enjoy! Why not interest other members of your family in home gardening? This way, you can not only divide the time needed to care for house plants, but also you can learn more by sharing the hobby with each other. Take my word, it won't be long before every member of your household wants to participate. By then, you can enjoy the status of "expert." Only, beware: gardening is one area in which experience is not necessarily the criterion for success. Some "upstart" in the household may be first time lucky!

C. With a large family such as yours, there are many reasons for home gardening. Plants are not only attractive, and an inexpensive way to decorate, they can also help out with the family food bill if you grow your own indoor vegetables, herbs, and fruits. And, for a busy mother, there are many indoor gardening projects that will keep children enthusiastically entertained.

19

a. Having young children in the family is a blessing, but sometimes it's easy to forget that after being indoors all day hearing, "What should I do now, Mommy?" Indoor gardening projects are a practical, educational and enjoyable solution to this query. You can teach children to assist with basic home gardening routines, such as watering and feeding. There is also a limitless store of creative projects that children will love. Just use your imagination, or let them use theirs! One possibility is a shoe planter. Take an old shoe, spray paint it, and mount it on a painted or lacquered board. Line the shoe with aluminum foil, fill it with potting soil, then set in your plant or plants and water them. You can also interest youngsters in gardening by giving them a sweet potato to grow. Select one with a lot of eyes, place toothpicks in its middle, suspend it in a jar or glass of water, and watch it grow! A miracle for a young child, and one which will capture his or her lifelong interest in growing things.

b. Since you do not have young children to worry about, you can experiment with many of the more delicate indoor gardening projects. Try your hand at a decorative terrarium. Or take a beautiful glass goblet and use multicolored layers of sand to create a picture visible through the glass. Plant small cacti on top. This will make a lovely decoration or gift, and the more you make, the better you become. Since you needn't worry about the wandering hands of children, you are also free to experiment with plants in unlikely spots, such as underneath a glass coffee table or along a staircase.

20

Plants, perhaps because they can't talk, enjoy the sounds of other living things around them now and then. Nature, what with the noise of insects, birds and animals, as well as the wind and water, isn't always peaceful and still.

a. Your quiet home, however, won't be a detriment to growing healthy and happy plants. Just let them share in when you're enjoying a good conversation or listening to television or radio.

b. You say your house is usually noisy. This can be good or bad depending on what you mean. Plants prefer a stable pattern of noise rather than constant surprises like "BOO" as someone jumps through a doorway. While yelling and hollering will not harm plants, screaming and bickering will. Vicious or vindicative quarreling will turn almost all plants into neurotic introverts, since anyone who is emotionally upset will more likely than not hurt their plants without meaning to, just by improper physical handling of the plant itself. Talk, don't touch—let the plant be a comfort, and not a recipient of your problems. And remember that plants need periods of rest and quiet, just as you do.

21

Cigarette, cigar or pipe exhaust can kill your plants. The smoke carries fine particles that collect on the leaves and clog up the pores, thus preventing your plant from breathing. It also blocks off the light, which is needed by plants for manufacturing food.

a. Do yourself and your plants a favor. Stop smoking, and convince everyone else who smokes that the habit isn't worth it. Smoke can kill a plant, and think what it does to your lungs! With smokers in the household, mist your plants frequently and wash their foliage once a week with a solution of biodegradable liquid dish soap and water. Too bad we can't so easily wash our lungs! Also, avoid touching plants after or while smoking. Otherwise, you might convey the tobacco mosaic virus to your plants. Petunias, pepper and tomato plants, to name a few, are susceptible to this disease. Washing your hands will prevent you from being the carrier.

b. I'm delighted for both you and your plants there are no smokers in your home. However, if guests who do smoke come over for a visit, keep your plants away from the ashtrays and seating arrangements. They, like you, are not accustomed to the smell or taste.

22

a. I call plants as presents "gifts that go on giving." Usually when we're given a house plant, there's no question of the plant receiving plenty of TLC. The question is, what kind and how much? Though it means a special effort on your part, I'd recommend stopping by a local florist, greenhouse or nursery to inquire about your new plant's needs. Even though you're not purchasing a plant, I think whomever you ask will be helpful. I've said before, good gardeners are made and not born. Even plants can't live on love alone. Before you introduce any new plant to his neighbors, check carefully for insects or disease. Prompt problem-solving will not only save the health of your new plant but prevent any trouble from spreading to your other plants.

b. As you're shopping for a plant, inquire about the care and growing conditions required by the varieties in which you are interested. As I've said many times, good gardeners are made and not born. Even plants can't live on love alone. Even if you're purchasing at a chain store or supermarket, the person in charge of the gardening or produce department should be able to give you some guidelines—if you'll just ask. Most florists and nurserymen, too, will be glad to answer questions if you stop by with your new purchase. As with all purchases, remember to look over what you're buying very carefully, checking for color, shape, turgidity, new growth, insects or fungas. Buy plants that have been properly "hardened off" and will withstand the change from greenhouse to your house. Delicate varieties are best purchased in the late spring or summer.

C. Whether your plants were gifts or purchases, the main question you should be concerned with is how to care for them properly. When you shop for a new plant, inquire about the care and growing conditions required by the varieties in which you're interested. Don't wait until you've already bought a plant to discover that it will not grow well in the area you've intended it for, that it has not been "hardened off" to withstand the transition from greenhouse to your home, or that it requires more attention than you have time to give it. Buy delicate varieties in the late spring or summer. As I've said many times before, good gardeners are made and not born. Even plants can't live on love alone. Most florists and nurserymen will be glad to answer questions if you stop by with your intended purchase. Even the person in charge of the gardening or produce department at a chain store or supermarket should be able to give you some guidelines—if you'll just ask. If you've received a new plant as a gift, it will save you effort and disappointment if you take the time to stop by a local florist, greenhouse or nursery to inquire about its needs. I think whomever you ask will be helpful, even if you are not purchasing there. Whether your new plant is a gift or purchase, check it over carefully for color, shape, turgidity, new growth, insects or fungus. The best time to problem-solve is before a new plant is brought into the house and introduced to new neighbors. When you do bring a new plant to your home, isolate it for a few days, gradually moving it nearer its final location. Plants need time to get used to new surroundings. Also, if they've been moved too roughly, or too suddenly to a new and different environment, they can suffer what we call "plant shock." In that case, they'll need rest and recuperation, too.

23

If I've caused you to pause and consider why you have house plants, I don't apologize. You'll never catch me saying plants aren't a responsibility like pets and children and family members. A light-hearted approach is necessary for enjoyment of home gardening, but this doesn't mean carelessness or neglect. I take my plant family seriously!

a. But since we agree house plants are enjoyable, here's to you, Green Thumber!

b. Plants do add something to the decor of any room, but plants suffering from lack of real care and interest won't look good for long. You know by now that you can't "shelve" a plant the way you can other objects around the house. So, if this is really the way you feel, you might consider finding a foster home with a horticulturist friend or donating your plants to a church or hospital, and substituting artificial greenery, which doesn't require the love and concern of the real thing.

C. The value of a gift is only what you place on it. You know by now you can't "shelve" a plant the way you can a Royal Doulton tea cup and saucer. So if this is what you'd really like to do, you might consider finding a foster home with a horticulturist friend or a church or hospital.

24

I'm willing to admit I like to talk. And to clear my "good" name, I've always said talking to plants is as therapeutic for you as for the plants. My suggestion that you talk to your plants is not meant to be magical, mystical, or nutty. Simply, when you take time out to talk as you work you have a tendency to be more gentle, observe more, and do a thorough job. Besides, don't you talk to the dog? As bright as either he or she may be, dogs really don't speak with words either.

Many studies have shown that plants like music and grow better when exposed to certain types of music. While I've read that plants withered and died after listening to rock and roll for three hours, the plants in my home are constantly exposed to the most violent collection of rock tunes available. Not only are there no adverse effects, but the plants seem to thrive on the sound. However, they do seem to relax a bit more in the evening when my wife and I listen to Montovani. Whatever the type of music, your plants will enjoy listening.

a. I'm so glad you agree with me, and I'm sure your plants are answering you with their vigorous growth. If not, why not try a new topic of conversation?

b. I've found that with much on my mind and lots happening in my life, having house plants named and displaying name tags helps slow me down long enough to appreciate each one as an individual. And though I haven't counted recently, my family's house plants must number three score. There's an old saying: what's in a name? Though I'd hardly make naming suggestions, as one who often forgets them, a name can be a game. Have you thought of naming your house plants after your grocer, broker, hairdresser, bootlegger, insurance man, etc? You'd have your services "at your fingertips!" I even know one young student who couldn't remember the names of the provinces of Canada for a forthcoming geography exam. One night she and her parents lined up their house plants and renamed them after each of the provinces.

After looking at those name tags for a week, that young lady got an A! You've already named your plant family, and every time you call your rubber plant "Roberto," you have a perfect reminder that your plant is more than an object —that he or she is a green pet, a confidant, and a friend.

c. You've been making your plants very happy with music. And I bet you've been enjoying it yourself. Keep it up!

d. You might want to try talking to your plants, naming them or playing music for their benefit. This may seem silly to you now, but just wait until you see the results in healthy new plant growth.

25

a. When you were a youngster, were you ever made to stand in the corner because you did something bad? Remember that feeling? Remember how you fidgeted? Well, plants get that same feeling when they must stay in one spot day in, day out. Though you may touch and turn them when you water and/or feed them, that's not enough. I suggest turning all potted plants once a day. The movement gives them the same exercise as a light breeze outdoors, and lets them know you're around. Most important, you will adjust their growth pattern by exposing all sides to the fixed light source. Plants enjoy an occasional change of scenery, and often look the better for a move, even if from one window to another. Just make sure that the lighting/humidity/temperature of the new area suits the needs of your plant. Plants become stiff when they've been inside all winter and enjoy a little exercise. Vibrate them occasionally by placing them on top of your radio or stereo speakers and let the base vibrations give them a "musical massage." Besides, they'll love the music.

b. Since you do vibrate your house plants, check the soil to make sure it hasn't become too compacted. The roots should have a bit of breathing space.

c. You already know this, judging by your answer. Why not have a revolving flowering centerpiece on your dining room table? As one plant flowers, place that one on the table or on the mantlepiece. When it begins to lose the blooms, have another plant, one which flowers later in the season, ready to replace it. This way you always have fresh flowers, and your plants have new views.

d. Why not touch, turn, vibrate, and move your plants? Think how dull you'd feel sitting still all day, day after day.

26

People often think that if they don't see insects or yellow or brown leaves, their plants are healthy. My criteria are much more stringent. Do your plants show new growth, and if so, where is it? When did you last see a bloom on your African violet or camellia? Does your spider plant have babies (new crowns) and did your poinsettia fire last year? Something can be done for most plant problems, if you care enough to analyze the health of your plant and realize there is a problem. The next step should be to consult an expert or a good book for the solution. However, discretion is most often the better part of valor. It is sometimes necessary to throw away a badly diseased plant, if only to save others from the same fate. For that you should never feel guilty.

a. I've never understood why not answering

or responding are considered not acting. If you do nothing about unhealthy house plants, you are doing something—the worst thing possible—resigning them to a slow (plants fight to live), painful death.

b. Discarding sick plants convinces me you really didn't want them around in the first place. The secret of success in growing healthy, happy plants is to practice the 3 p's: Pride, Patience and Persistence. Sometimes these three simple rules of thumb are a real test, but no one ever said that being an indoor gardener was easy.

c. Realizing you have an unhealthy house plant is the first step in the right direction, and I'm glad to see you've taken it. Since you care enough to check for problems, I'm sure you can cure them. The main criterion is that you are interested in the welfare of your plants.

d. Realizing you have an unhealthy house plant is the first step in the right direction, and I'm glad to see you've taken it. If you're lucky enough to have a horticulturist as spouse or friend, their expert advice can be a great savings! Remember, though, you know your house plants best, and you're the one who should be most sensitive to their well-being. There are often similar symptoms for different problems, so if the recommended solution doesn't work, re-check the cause and try something else.

27

A regular feeding program for your house plants is as important as a watering regimen— even for those house plants growing in water. Believe it or not, the plant foods you find on the market are there for a reason. Why? Remember that the plants in your home have their origins in the great outdoors where Mother Nature used to take care of their nutritional needs. In your home, it's up to you to be Mother Nature and supply your indoor plants with a properly balanced natural diet since they cannot derive it from the earth in a natural environment themselves. What kind of plant food? Unless you'd like to donate a kitchen cabinet or basement shelf to storing the vast array of house plant foods in all shapes, sizes and forms now on the market, I recommend stocking an all-purpose natural plant food safe for all indoor plants that contains the three basic fertilizer ingredients: nitrogen, which aids in growing strong, healthy foliage; phosphorous, which is a root builder; and potash, which promotes flowering. Since most plants, with the exception of the carnivore family, don't have mouths with which to handle solid food, they digest whatever food and nutrients you feed them as they are dissolved in water. Therefore, I've found that liquid plant foods are easiest to measure and dissolve in a solution. I like to keep things simple, and if you do also, try using a liquid that measures itself—you know, a capful to a quarter of water, or some other simple routine. That way, you can feed as regularly as you water, without waiting for your plants to scream at you for food by looking sickly. However, I'm never heavy handed with plant food. I use only the manufacturer's recommended amount, because plants, like people and pets, become sluggish if overfed, and a "stuffed" house plant may produce lush foliage, but it will never bloom! Depending upon the soil your house plants are potted in, they may also need periodic iron supplements, especially in early winter and late spring. Micronized iron is available in the horticultural section of most stores, or you can insert a rusty nail or two in the soil of your pots.

a. If you're feeding your plants once a day, you are over doing it. Even most water-loving plants are given a chance to dry out a bit, and your plants especially need time to digest their food.

b. Once-a-week feeding is fine if you use a water-soluble fertilizer properly diluted.

c. While a once-a-month feeding, as you've been doing, is recommended by some gardening specialists, I feel more frequent feeding with a water soluble fertilizer is preferable. You don't like to stuff yourself at one meal and then have to wait on an empty stomach for the next feast, and neither do your plants. Regular meals are more healthy and satisfying.

d. If you feed your house plants only four times a year, you're letting your friends go hungry. Encourage growth by feeding more often with a water soluble plant fertilizer.

e. While it's true that plants make their own

food from the sunlight, they still need certain elements not available in their potted condition, from the soil, the light or the water. These elements are found in house plant fertilizers. So don't let your plants go hungry. Feed regularly with a water soluble plant food.

28

My rule of thumb on watering, you ask? I don't have one. I use my whole hand! I water when the soil is dry to the touch, and I keep my shade-loving house plants always damp, but never soggy wet. If you're uncertain about your judgement, however, there are several inexpensive but reliable water indicators now on the market. One just turns blue when yor plant needs watering; another acts as an automatic watering wick and feeds water into the soil as required. For most plants, except cacti and succulents, water well when you do water. The soil should be moistened through and through until water trickles out of the drainage holes in the bottom of your pots. When the pot drips, you know you've done a thorough job. When watering from the top, you can avoid making holes in the soil by placing a small, flat stone on top of the soil and pouring the water over it. Some gardeners are adamant about which way to water—from the top, or from the bottom. To my mind, it makes no difference, as long as the amount of water supplied is adequate. I do recommend watering during the daylight hours when your plants, like you, are most active, respiring rapidly. Hanging baskets can be inconvenient to water. A trick I've found handy is to water plants in hanging baskets with ice cubes in a styrofoam cup that has holes punched in its bottom so that ice water, as it melts, can run through. Using a styrofoam cup rather than a plain paper one will keep the cold from the ice cubes insulated in the cup, and because the watering this way is so gradual, your plants won't suffer cold water shock. Moreover, with this method, there's no drip or mess.

a. If you are watering once a day, you are overdoing it. All plants should be given a chance to dry out a bit.

b. Watering once a week may be fine—for some of your plants. For others you are causing problems by over or under watering. These problems can be easily avoided by treating your plants as the individuals they are, and using the touch-tell test or a water indicator.

c. Congratulations, because you know that dry soil is the best method of deciding when to water. But remember that certain types of plants, such as the philodendron and fern families, prefer moist soil, while plants that are resting require a bit less water than usual.

29

a. The humidity in your home will determine whether your plants need one or more showers a day, a week, or a month. Plants in dry, warm rooms will need more frequent mistings than plants in cool, damp rooms. Most plants, however, enjoy a daily misting with warm, pure water. The major exceptions to this rule are foliage and flowering plants with fuzzy, velvety leaves, such as African violets and gloxinias, which don't like bathing, and cacti and succulents, accustomed to a dry environment in nature. In addition to mistings regularly, I sometimes give my plants a real treat—a steam bath. To do this, place your plant on a brick or stone in a pail of hot water. Make sure the water level in the pail is lower than the height of the brick so the bottom of the pot isn't sitting in the hot water. Allow the plant to soak up the moisture for five minutes or so, and then remove it, being especially careful to keep it out of drafts until it readjusts to room temperature again.

b. Clean plants are happy plants. Wash them as often as they need it, usually once or twice a month, by hand, with paper towels, or as I do, using a small-sized hand sprayer designed for indoor plants. Either way, bathe them with a solution of two teaspoons liquid biodegradable dish soap per half gallon room temperature water. Wipe or spray the foliage top and bottom, and then rinse with clear, pure room-temperature water to remove all leftover soap. I usually rinse with a cupful of weak tea added to the rinse water, which acts as an astringent and deepens the color of the foliage. For plants which are uncomfortable with wet foliage, such as African violets and gloxinias, dust the foliage with a soft, camel hair brush.

c. If your plants are sick from insects or a disease, you should spray or dust them with a proper medication, but never spray or dust as a preventative. Do you take an aspirin to prevent a headache? If you do need to use an insecticide or other remedy, follow directions carefully, and be as concerned about your plants' reaction to the treatment as you are—I hope—when you are taking medications.

30

a. Good potting soil is absolutely essential for all plants, though each type of plant has its own preferences. Why not? We all have different tastes in food and clothing. Whatever kind of soil you use, it should be approximately 50% solid by volume, and 50% porous. Like many other practiced home gardeners, I've found that the commercially packaged potting soils are too dense to allow for good drainage when used alone, but they work fine if mixed with a lighter material, such as screened compost, milled sphagnum moss, sand or gravel, in varying amounts, depending upon what you're planting. The philodendron family, for instance, grows well in heavy soil, as do such specialty plants as azaleas and cyclamens. African violets and cacti, on the other hand, must have a light soil, with a high percentage of sand and/or gravel mixed in. None the less, good drainage for all plants, which allows air pockets to be formed in the soil, is the most important consideration of your house plants' immediate growing environment. Without it, even a proper watering routine will be of no avail. Your plants will suffocate. If you're a newcomer to home gardening, try mixing up a number of different soils before you plant and test them to see how they hold water and compress. Back to nature? Start with the earth!

b. Good potting soil is absolutely essential for all plants, though each type of plant has its own preferences. Why not? We all have different tastes in food and clothing. Since you've been mixing your own potting soils, you may have your own secrets of what works best for the kinds of plants you grow. To share some of my own secrets, though, my rule of thumb is that any good soil should be approximately 50% solid by volume, and 50% porous. A good all-purpose potting soil, enjoyed by geraniums, amaryllis, dracaenas, oxalis and palms, for example, combines two parts garden soil, one part compost or leaf mold, and one part sand. For plants that like a high humus content, such as African violets, begonias, philodendrons and azaleas, I pot them in a mixture of equal parts of sand, peat moss, garden soil and compost. Cacti and succulents prosper best in a mixture of one part garden soil, one part sand, and a half part crushed clay pot or brick, especially if you add in a pinch of bonemeal and a pinch of horticultural limestone. To sterilize a "home brew," heat the soil in trays in your oven to a temperature between 200°-212°, but no higher or the plants will not grow in the soil. Depending upon the heaviness of the soil you're preparing, it will have to take from 15-40 minutes to reach just over 200° in temperature.

31

How many times have you heard the old saying, "If your feet hurt, you hurt all over?" Shoes play a great part in the comfort of both people and plants. Yes, plants wear shoes. Why not? Since plants' roots are their feet, plants' pots are their shoes. They should always start out with shoes that fit and move up one size at a time when their toes grow out of the holes in the bottom of their shoes. As everyday work shoes, however, plants prefer porous shoes that breathe to decorative haberdashery. Porous pots allow moisture to evaporate through the pot walls. This keeps plant roots cooler when the temperature is high. The reverse is also true. A porous pot picks up humidity, keeping the soil damp during dry periods. In choosing planters, remember that the plant should not have to compete with the pot for attention.

b, c, e. Plants that are potted in ceramic, china, plastic or metal containers may look beautifully dressed, but they feel as uncomfortable as a child in Sunday clothes would during a sunny day at the beach. Why not replant your flowered and foliage friends in clay, wood or pottery? You can always set the plant, work shoes and all, inside a fancier container, on top of about an inch or two of pebbles. Leave one to one-and-a-half inches of air space all around the inner pot.

a, d. With clay or wood pots, your plants are perfectly dressed for a comfortable life. If you'd like to dress them up occasionally, then use one of the decorative pots. Only buy it large enough so that the wood or clay container fits inside with at least one to one-and-a-half inches of air space all around. This way, as your plant grows, all you'll need to buy is new everyday shoes. Never set large wooden tubs directly on the ground or floor, or the bottom of the tub will decay. Promote good drainage by raising the tub off the floor with bricks or other supports.

3²

Pots with holes in the bottom are good for all house plants, and essential for the health and well-being of many, especially those plants requiring a lot of water. Good drainage depends on excess water escaping from the soil around the roots and air being able to penetrate the soil. I'd urge you to make sure a few small pieces of broken pottery or a smattering of gravel are in the bottom of each pot. An additional function of drainage holes is that they tell you when your plant needs repotting —when the roots begin poking through the holes.

a. Though you've indicated your plants are housed in pots with holes, should you sometime acquire a planter without a drainage vent, make sure this protective drainage layer of pottery pieces or gravel or a mixture of both is there.

Check occasionally to make sure watering hasn't caused the soil to pack down the drainage holes.

b. You might consider repotting your plants, putting a broken shard or two or a smattering of gravel in the bottom of each pot with a hole, or else drill a few small holes in the bottom of your pots without drainage holes. If you are happiest using pots or planters without drainage holes, then it is absolutely essential that you have this drainage layer of pottery pieces or gravel or a mixture of both.

c. Your plants potted in containers with holes should be just fine, especially with a bottom layer of the pottery pieces and gravel. For those plants that do not have aerated "shoes," you might consider repotting them in containers with drainage holes, or drilling holes in the pots you do have. If not, at least have a layer of pottery pieces or gravel or a mixture of both on the bottom of the pot.

33

An underliner is a separate saucer or tray kept underneath the plant pot. Gravel or charcoal-filled underliners (my preference is a mixture of 2/3 stones, 1/3 charcoal) serve multiple purposes. If you keep the water level halfway up the stones, never touching the pots, you'll ensure that your plants' roots don't rot and they can breathe. At the same time, the evaporation will provide a direct source of moisture for your plants. Underliners of this sort will also allow a run-off if you've overwatered from the top. They also prevent damage to furniture and rugs. And if you've used my mixture of 1/3 charcoal, you'll also have installed an "automatic" air freshener! I recommend washing the stones once a month with soap and water to eliminate any foreign growth or bacteria.

a. Since you use an underliner you already

know the benefits. If you aren't using this gravel/ charcoal mixture, try it—you'll like it!

b. This is as good a time as any to begin using an underliner. The advantages are undeniable.

34

a. The green moss on the sides, edges or surface of the soil or pot means you are placing the pots too close together and are keeping the soil too damp. To remove the moss, add a tablespoon of bleach to soapy water, and scrub the sides of the pot. Spoon out mossy soil, and replace with fresh, sterile all-purpose house plant soil or gardening mix. Check for proper drainage and ventilation, and thereafter watch your water! Since this green scum might be a form of algae that grows on unused fertilizer, make sure you aren't overfeeding.

b. If you see your pots or surface of the soil covered with white crystals, you've got a salt flat. Filter your water through charcoal and place a layer of charcoal on top of the soil. A grayish-white powdery coating, however, is mildew. Dusting with sulfur will cure the disease; proper air circulation will prevent it in the first place.

C. Since you've indicated you've not noticed green moss, white crystals, or grayish powder on your pots or the surface of your house plants' soil, you've avoided three of the most common house plant illnesses: moss or fungus growth, salt formations, and mildew. Keep on doing what you're doing.

35

You might think that house plants, being indoors, unless you summer your plants outside, would be free from insects. On the contrary, as ants or mosquitos are able to penetrate your home, so do house plant-loving insects manage to find their way in. Most damage to house plants is done by sucking insects, which draw sap from the plants and interrupt normal growth and propagation.

a. Your problem with foliage insects should disappear if you add a pinch of malathion to the soap and water solution with which you wash your foliage.

b. Soil and stem insects can be controlled by sprinkling a light amount of 10% chlordane ant powder, or some similar substance, on the surface of the soil. These commercial insecticides are available at any garden supply center. Check the labels carefully for directions.

c, d, e. Curled leaves, mold, or holes in the leaves are all signs of insect invasion. The first thing you should do is wash your plant carefully with biodegradable dishwashing soap and water. Cotton swabs dipped in alcohol will rid your plants of some common pests. You may need an insecticide, such as malathion, in which case you should read the labels to find the right one for your plant and its problem, then follow the application instructions.

f. While I applaud your indicating your house plants are insect free, I caution you to keep up your vigilance. Be curious. Do you notice something that wasn't there yesterday? Your plants will like the extra attention.

36

From time to time, every plant parent has a "problem child" going through an awkward growth stage. Problems with the shape of your house plants are usually the result of too much or too little or misdirected lighting.

a. If your plants' foliage is sparse on extended stems, chances are the lighting—natural or artificial—is inadequate. Try moving the plant, or extending its hours of daylight. If the plant leans, it's reaching for the light source. Turn it often, at least once a day, so it will grow straight.

b. Thick foliage on short stems indicates the intensity of light is too strong. Move the plant back, or change its location. If a plant leans, it's reaching out for the light source. Turn it each day so it will grow straight.

c. You seem to have found the right locations for your plants and are turning them regularly so they are full and straight. Great!

37

There are several main possibilities for any plant problem—watering, feeding, temperature, lighting, insects and diseases. If you carefully review your system of plant care, you'll probably be able to correct bad situations now, before any new problems develop. However, if you notice that something is not right now, and you can't decide what caused it, go over each possibility, one by one—I think you'll find the answer. And never hesitate to consult an expert, either through a good book on plant care, or better yet, in person. They wouldn't be experts unless they loved plants, and anyone who loves plants wants to see them healthy.

a. Scaly or cracked, withered foliage on a plant is a sign of dehydration. I highly recommend that you mist the foliage daily with a light spray of pure water and/or a weak tea solution, and that you give your plant the sauna steam bath I've told you about earlier. Just watering isn't enough. If you try to compensate by over-watering for what is really a humidity problem, you'll drown your plant with good intentions.

b. Light green leaves that have dark green veins the color of which the whole leaf should be means that your plant is suffering from chlorosis. This means that the plant is anemic and needs more iron. Give the patient a healthy dose of iron, followed by a small meal. This problem is caused by too much strong light or wetting of the leaves. Move the plant to a shaded area.

c. If you notice beads of moisture on the surface of the foliage, your plant has a cold. Stop feeding it and cover the surface of the soil with plant charcoal. Water if the plant is dry, but not if it is damp. Wash with soap and water and rinse with mild tea. And say, "Gold Bless You" if necessary.

38

Losing leaves is perhaps the most dramatic sign of something you've done wrong. Leaves falling off can be caused by cold drafts, which we've discussed how to avoid, but it is primarily a function of improper watering.

a. Since you've indicated your house plants are losing leaves from the top, I'd suggest being a little more heavy handed with the watering can from now on, and checking to make sure there's sufficient humidity. Please…for plant's sake… review the watering advice I gave you!!!

b. Since you've indicated your house plants are losing leaves from the middle to lower mature foliage, I'd suggest being lighter handed with the watering can from now on. Check, too, to make sure your plants have proper drainage and ventilation, and are housed in the right sized pots.

And please...for plant's sake...review the watering advice I gave you!!!

C. Since you've indicated your house plants are not losing any leaves, you must be gaining them. Here's to you!!!

39

The color of your house plants' foliage is dependent upon your feeding care.

a. If your foliage is rich and bright in color, you seem to have found the comfortable level of nutrients for each of your plants. As I said earlier, stick to your regimen.

b. If your foliage seems off-color or faded, the right amount of nutrients aren't being supplied. If new, young foliage is pale yellowish (assuming the natural color of the plant isn't yellow), your plant needs iron. If mature foliage turns grayish, your plant wants food. Careful, however of flowering house plants. If you overfeed them, they'll reward you with lush foliage, but never bloom. Yellow or bleached leaves might also be due to improper watering. If the lower extremities are yellow, you probably aren't watering enough. Other causes of yellow leaves are improper lighting or too small a pot.

40

The conditions of the leaf tips of your plants indicates how well the plants like their locations.

a. When the ends of the leaves turn brown, it means your plants are uncomfortble in a warm, dry draft. Find out where the draft is coming from by using a lit candle and watching which way the flame bends. If nothing can be done about the draft, you'll have to move the plant.

b. When the ends of the leaves turn black, your plants are uncomfortable in a cold draft. Find out where the draft is coming from by using a lit candle and watching which way the flame bends. If nothing can be done about the draft, you'll have to move the plant.

c. If the ends of the leaves are consistent in color(s) with the foliage of the plant in general, you can be sure your plants are out of the way of hot or cold drafts.

41

Firm, alert foliage is the sign of a healthy, happy, well-watered and well-fed plant.

a. You'll know you are entitled to several "pluses" for good house plant care if the foliage of your plants is turgid, bright and vibrant.

b. If your foliage droops or turns under, rush water, for starters, then reconsider your whole house plant care regimen. Wilting or drooping is often caused by lack of humidity, as well as by improper watering. Remember: too much of anything is at least as bad as too little!

c. If you've been noticing brown or black spots on your foliage plants, take another look at the way you water. Are you splashing your sensitive plants with cold water? It looks that way.

d. Dull foliage is often the result of air quality. Try frequent washing, misting and dusting with a clean cloth. You can always purchase one of the products designed to give your leaves a shine, but if you do, be very careful. Plants breathe through their leaves as we do through our skin.